First World War
and Army of Occupation
War Diary
France, Belgium and Germany

19 DIVISION
Headquarters, Branches and Services
Royal Army Ordnance Corps
Deputy Assistant Director Ordnance Services
2 September 1915 - 27 January 1919

WO95/2066/2

The Naval & Military Press Ltd
www.nmarchive.com
Published in association with The National Archives

Published by

The Naval & Military Press Ltd

Unit 10 Ridgewood Industrial Park,

Uckfield, East Sussex,

TN22 5QE England

Tel: +44 (0) 1825 749494

www.naval-military-press.com

www.nmarchive.com

This diary has been reprinted in facsimile from the original. Any imperfections are inevitably reproduced and the quality may fall short of modern type and cartographic standards.

© **Crown Copyright**
Images reproduced by permission of The National Archives, London, England, 2015.

Contents

Document type	Place/Title	Date From	Date To
Heading	WO95/2066/2 19 Div HQ 1915 July-1919 Feb D A D O S		
Heading	D.A.D.O.S. Jly 1915-Feb 1919		
Heading	Hq Coy. 19th Div D.A.D.O.S. Vol I July & August 15		
Heading	19th Division Diary Of D.A.D.O.S. For August 1915		
Miscellaneous	Diary Of D.A.D.O.S. 19th Division	04/09/1915	04/09/1915
Heading	HQ Co. 19th Div D.A.D.O.S. Vol II Sept 15		
Heading	War Diary Of D.A.D.O.S. 19th Division. From 1st Sept. 1915 To 30th Sept 1915		
War Diary		02/09/1915	30/09/1915
Heading	War Diary Of D.A.D.O.S. 19th Division From 1st To 31st Oct R 1915 Vol 3		
War Diary		01/10/1915	30/10/1915
Heading	H.Q. 19th Div D.A.D.R. Vol 4 Nov 15		
Heading	War Diary Of D.A.D.O.S. 19th Division From 1st November 1915 To 30th Nov 1915		
War Diary		01/11/1915	30/11/1915
Heading	D.A.D.O.S. 19th Div. Vol 5 Dec 1915		
Heading	War Diary Of D.A.D.O.S. 19th Division From 1st To 31st December 1915		
War Diary		01/12/1915	30/12/1915
Heading	D.A.D.O.S. 19th Div Vol 6		
Heading	War Diary Of D A D O S 19th Division From 1st To 31st January 1916		
War Diary		01/01/1916	31/01/1916
Heading	War Diary Of D A D O S 19th Division From 1st To 29th February 1916		
War Diary		03/02/1916	29/02/1916
Heading	War Diary Of D A D O S 19th Division From 1st To 31st March 1916		
War Diary		01/03/1916	31/03/1916
Heading	War Diary Of D.A.D.O.S. 19th Division From 1st To 30th April 1916		
War Diary		01/04/1916	30/04/1916
Heading	War Diary Of D.A.D.O.S. 19th Division From 1st To 31st May 1916		
War Diary		01/05/1916	31/05/1916
Heading	War Diary Of D A D O S 19th Division From 1st To 30th June 1916		
War Diary		01/06/1916	29/06/1916
Heading	War Diary Of D.A.D.O.S. 19th Division. From 1st To 31st July 1916		
War Diary		01/07/1916	31/07/1916
Heading	War Diary Of D A D O S 19th Division From 1st To 31st August 1916		
War Diary		02/08/1916	31/08/1916
Heading	War Diary Of D.A.D.O.S. 19th Division. From 1st To 30th September. 1916.		
War Diary		05/09/1916	30/09/1916

Heading	War Diary Of D A D O S 19th Division From 1st To 31st October 1916 Vol 15		
War Diary		02/10/1916	31/10/1916
Heading	War Diary Of D.A.D.O.S. 19th Division. From 1st To 30th November. 1916 Vol 16		
War Diary		01/11/1916	30/11/1916
Heading	War Diary Of D.A.D.O.S. 19th Division From 1st To 31st December. 1916		
War Diary		01/12/1916	28/12/1916
Heading	War Diary Of D.A.D.O.S. 19th Division From 1st To 31st January 1917 Vol 18		
War Diary		01/01/1917	21/01/1917
Heading	War Diary Of D.A.D.O.S. 19th Division From 1st To 28th February. 1917 Vol 19		
War Diary		02/02/1917	23/02/1917
Heading	War Diary Of D.A.D.O.S. 19th Division. From 1st To 31st March 1917 Vol 20		
War Diary		01/03/1917	31/03/1917
Heading	War Diary Of D.A.D.O.S. 19th Division. From 1st To 30th April 1917 Vol 21		
War Diary		02/04/1917	27/04/1917
Heading	War Diary Of D.A.D.O.S. 19th Division From 1st To 31st May 1917 Vol 22		
War Diary		02/05/1917	29/05/1917
Heading	War Diary Of D.A.D.O.S. 19th Division From 1st To 30th June 1917 Vol 23		
War Diary		01/06/1917	30/06/1917
Heading	War Diary Of D.A.D.O.S. 19th Division. From 1st To 31 July 1917 Vol 24		
War Diary		02/07/1917	31/07/1917
Heading	War Diary Of D.A.D.O.S. 19th Division. From 1st To 31st August 1917 Vol 25		
War Diary		01/08/1917	29/08/1917
Heading	War Diary Of D.A.D.O.S. 19th Division From 1st To 30th September 1917 Vol 26		
War Diary		03/09/1917	27/09/1917
Heading	War Diary Of D.A.D.O.S. 19th Division From 1st To 31st October 1917 Vol 27		
War Diary		02/10/1917	30/10/1917
Heading	War Diary Of D.A.D.O.S 19th Division. From 1st To 30th November 1917 Vol 28		
War Diary		01/11/1917	29/11/1917
Heading	War Diary Of D.A.D.O.S. 19th Division From 1st To 31st December 1917 Vol 29		
War Diary		01/12/1917	24/12/1917
Heading	War Diary Of D.A.D.O.S. 19th Division From 1st To 31st January 1918 Vol 30		
War Diary		01/01/1918	29/01/1918
Heading	War Diary Of D.A.D.O.S. 19th Division From 1st To 28th February 1918 Vol 31		
War Diary		06/02/1918	23/02/1918
Heading	War Diary Of D.A.D.O.S. 19th Division From 1st To 31st March 1918 Vol 32		
War Diary		04/03/1918	31/03/1918
Heading	War Diary Of D.A.D.O.S. 19th Division From 1st To 30th April 1918 Vol 33		

War Diary		01/04/1918	30/04/1918
Heading	War Diary Of D.A.D.O.S 19th Division From 1st To 31st May 1918 Vol 34		
War Diary		01/05/1918	31/05/1918
Heading	War Diary Of D.A.D.O.S 19th Division From 1st To 30th June 1918 Vol 35		
War Diary		02/06/1918	27/06/1918
Heading	War Diary Of D.A.D.O.S 19th Division From 1st To 31st July 1918 Vol 36		
War Diary		04/07/1918	26/07/1918
Heading	War Diary Of D.A.D.O.S. 19th Division From 1st To 31st August 1918 Vol 37		
War Diary		01/08/1918	29/08/1918
Heading	War Diary Of D.A.D.O.S 19th Division From 1st To 30th September 1918 Vol 38		
War Diary		02/09/1918	28/09/1918
Heading	War Diary Of D.A.D.O.S. 19th Division From 1st To 31st October 1918 Vol 39		
War Diary		01/10/1918	31/10/1918
Heading	War Diary Of D.A.D.O.S. 19th Division From 1st To 30th November 1918 Vol 40		
War Diary		01/11/1918	28/11/1918
Miscellaneous	War Diary Of D.A.D.O.S. 19th Division From 1st To 31st December 1918 Vol 41		
War Diary		06/12/1918	21/12/1918
Heading	War Diary Of D.A.D.O.S. 19th Division From 1st To 31st January 1919 Vol 42		
War Diary		15/01/1919	27/01/1919
Heading	War Diary Of D.A.D.O.S. 19th Division From 1st To 28th February 1919 Vol 43		
War Diary			

WO 95
2066/2

19 Div
HQ

1915 July - 1919 Feb
DADOS

19TH DIVISION

D. A. D. O. S.
JLY 1915-FEB 1919

19TH DIVISION

121/6787

19th Division

"4th Aus: 19th Div:
to S.S. & S.
Vol. I

July & August 15

Feb '19

Bean

19th Division
Diary of D.A.D.M.S.
for August. 1915.

Diary of D.A.D.O.S. 19th Division

Date	Arros.	Date	Note
August 20th	Received goggles for R.A. also smoke helmets for R.A. horses	July 17th	Arrived at Boulogne
" 22nd	Further supply of satchels smoke helmets received; also bivery lamps for Infantry Bns.	" 18th	Rejoined Unit
		" 24th	Passed night at Jouves - Samomake helmets received
" 23rd	Laid hold of 57th Brigade L. Homd. for smoke helmets.	" 29th	Depôt opened at Samerie. Rifle rests drawn from return near 17th Rd supply column
" 29th	Received first lot bokophoscant night sights to catapults and time loose reserve, 300 rifle covers	" 30th	Wire telescope rifles received, the received to each Infantry Bn.
" 24th	Received from the Rayonpeld Workshops 3000 bands for smoke helmets	" 31st	First consignment of Smith general service also respirators for reserve
" 29th	Received 209 tube smoke helmets	August 2nd	13 Lewis M.Guns arrived to complete Bris to 4 each
" 30th	Received Stable illuminating tench	" 11th	Checker Newspedder received and
" 31st	Moved to cow.		Received 2nd to 79th Fd
		" 7th	5250 Smoke helmets received
	W Smith Capt. D.A.D.O.S 19th Div.	" 8th	Respirators sent forward for 2nd smoke helmets of Batln; part consignment of newly opened helmets received
		" 9th	Balance of Smoke helmets to complete reserve received
Locou 11.9.15.		" 10th	3 Boots Trousers 111 Catapults taken over from Special Division
		" 12th	Bought 75 pairs half lees at Locon for issue to Brigade Shoemakers Shop
		" 13th	Received seats for protecting arming case of S.R. service? guns
		" 15th	Arranged purchase of cloth for rifle covers Started at of Tulse smoke helmets received. Also small supply of patches
		" 19th	Large consignment of boots received first issue to Brigade Shoemakers Shops D.A.D.O.S Army created Office

12/6930

19th Kwanw

H.D. Ono: 19th Dir.
BABOL
Vol. II

Sept. 15

CONFIDENTIAL

WAR DIARY
OF
D.A.D.O.S. 19th DIVISION.

From 1st Sept. 1915, To 30th Sept. 1915.

(Capt. W. Smith. A.O.D.)

WAR DIARY
or
INTELLIGENCE SUMMARY

(Erase heading not required.)

Army Form C. 2118

Instructions regarding War Diaries and Intelligence Summaries are contained in F.S. Regs., Part II. and the Staff Manual respectively. Title Pages will be prepared in manuscript.

Place	Date	Hour	Summary of Events and Information	Remarks and references to Appendices
	Sept 1915			
	2nd		Received 15 Vermorel Sprayers	W.S.
	4th		Received 1980 Tube Pattern Smoke Helmets	W.S.
	6th		Received 1584 " " " " , and 1900 Blankets	W.S.
	7th		Received 6 Drums of Blankets	W.S.
	10th		Received 90 Winchester covered bottles H.B. fills from B.P. for use in Trenches	W.S.
	11th		Received 10 Electric Signalling Lamps, 15 Cases Hypo Smoke Helmets, 61 Chests of Rifles (not for H.V. Ammn)	W.S.
			and 1 Case of Bayonets, also 250 Vigilant Periscopes.	W.S.
	12th		Received 20 Bicycles	W.S.
	13th		Received 2000 Tube Smoke Helmets	W.S.
	15th		Received 34 Periscopes No 9	W.S.
	16th		" " 1500 Tube Smoke Helmets	W.S.
	17th		" " 2000 " " " "	W.S.
	18th		Received 500 Stabbing Weapons	W.S.
			" " 1000 Tube Smoke Helmets	W.S.
	19th		4 Carriages Ambulance Stretchers 50 Bayonets Scabs, and 400 Round Patches	W.S.
	20th		one gun reported unserviceable "C" Batty 88"Bty RFA, wired Base Commander for replacing	W.S.
	21st		" " "A" " " " " " "	W.S.
	22nd		Received 1834 Tube Smoke Helmets.	W.S.

Army Form C. 2118

WAR DIARY
or
INTELLIGENCE SUMMARY
(Erase heading not required.)

Instructions regarding War Diaries and Intelligence Summaries are contained in F. S. Regs., Part II. and the Staff Manual respectively. Title Pages will be prepared in manuscript.

Place	Date	Hour	Summary of Events and Information	Remarks and references to Appendices
	Sept 1915			
	23rd		Received 85 Vermorel Sprayers, Wind Vane, hanging Lamps, machine gun parts	A03
	25th		Received 2 gun 18 pdrs, 6 lamps Electric Signalling and 2 Barometers Aneroid	A05
	26th		Received 2950 Goggles Anti gas and 767 Badges grenade	A05
	27th		Reported Rifle S.B. required 100 Rifles in July, there were obtained from R.O.O. Armentières	A05
	30th		Received Russian machine gun parts issued for 23.9.15, 2 Telescopic Rifles from O.O. Indian Corps troops and 34 Bicycles from Base.	A05

W Smith Captain.
D.A.D.O.S. 1st Division

19th Division

CONFIDENTIAL

/21/
7432

WAR DIARY
OF
D.A.D.O.S. 19TH DIVISION.

FROM 1ST TO 31ST OCTR 1915

Vol: 3.

Army Form C. 2118

WAR DIARY
or
INTELLIGENCE SUMMARY
(Erase heading not required.)

Instructions regarding War Diaries and Intelligence Summaries are contained in F. S. Regs., Part II. and the Staff Manual respectively. Title Pages will be prepared in manuscript.

Place	Date	Hour	Summary of Events and Information	Remarks and references to Appendices
	Oct/10/15			
	1st		Received 20 Periscopes 412 q in lieu of 412 14	MS.
	2nd		Moved to G.A.Tme., 36 too Indn pattern Anvoid Helmets received	MS.
	4th		100 Antigas goggles received, and sent to 12 Corps troops	MS.
	5th		2 Rifles with Telescopic Sights received from D.O. Ind. Corps troops	MS.
	6th		Received 1400 Rifle Covers and 2 Rifles with Telescopic Sights	MS.
	7th		Received 68 Periscopes No. q, and 500 Vigilant	MS.
	8th		Received Belts Woollen 19,994, Vests Woollen 2000, Drawers Woollen 10,000, Periscopes No. q - 78, Elmn. J.b. 6 galls 60	MS.
	9th		Received 10,000 Drawers Woollen	MS.
	10th		Received 210 Trench Stretchers	MS.
	11th		Received Carriage Amb. & Stretcher 5, Cun J.b. 6 galls 70, and Striking Weapons 200.	MS.
	12th		Received Goggles Antigas 1300, Drawers Woollen 10,000 and Dinis Aiguelling 152	MS.
	13th		Received 3 Rifles with Telescopic Sights	MS.
	14th		Received 2000 pr Drawers Woollen, 7 Lamps Electric 4th Aiguelling, and 1 Lewis Machine gun	MS.
	15th		Received 100 Antigas Goggles	MS.
	16th		Received 96 Strikes Indicator Fuze 18 pr.	MS.
	17th		Received 100 Steel Helmets and 2000 Vests Woollen	MS.
	18th		Received 100 Brasserie 5 galls, and 1 Lewis Machine gun	MS.

Army Form C. 2118

WAR DIARY
or
INTELLIGENCE SUMMARY
(Erase heading not required.)

Instructions regarding War Diaries and Intelligence Summaries are contained in F. S. Regs., Part II. and the Staff Manual respectively. Title Pages will be prepared in manuscript.

Place	Date Oct 1915	Hour	Summary of Events and Information	Remarks and references to Appendices
	20th		Received 3000 Goggles Antigas	MS.
	21st		Moved to Scorran. Received 1800 Vests Woollen, 144 Cowwellers Limbering, 6108 Bomb Carrier 14035 Rifle Cover	MS.
	22nd		Received 1000 Rug Horse and 13.000 Caper waterintosh	MS.
	23rd		Received 1800 Rug Horse, 1500 Antigas goggles and 5 Carriage Ambulance Stretcher	MS.
	24th		Received 6 Lamps Electric Field Signalling and 1,500 Antigas goggles	MS.
	25th		Received 40 Pannier Signalling 1000 Vests Woollen, 700 Coats Sleeperkin lined and 1 Lewis gun from Base before Div	MS.
	27th		Received 2 Barometer Aneroid, 2000 Antigas goggles, and 6 Kennard Sprayers	MS.
	28th		Received 2675 Gloves Fingerless, 1088 prs Gum Boots and 16 Vermorel Sprayers	MS.
	29th		Received 35 Veils for Snipers & Observers	MS.
	30th		Received 500 Vests Woollen, 1300 goggles Antigas and 80 tents C.S.E.	MS.

W. Smith Captain
D.A.D.S.S. 19th Division

Hq. 19th Div.
Staffs.
Vol. 4

121/7678

Nov 15.

CONFIDENTIAL

War Diary
of
D.A.D.O.S., 19th Division.

From 1st November 1915 To 30th Nov. 1915

Army Form C. 2118

WAR DIARY
or
INTELLIGENCE SUMMARY
(Erase heading not required.)

Instructions regarding War Diaries and Intelligence Summaries are contained in F. S. Regs., Part II. and the Staff Manual respectively. Title Pages will be prepared in manuscript.

Place	Date Nov 1915	Hour	Summary of Events and Information	Remarks and references to Appendices
	1st		Received 2304 pair of Gum Boots	NS
	2nd		Received 14,902 Undercoats Fur, of which 1902 were returned to D. Paris	NS
	3rd		Issued 2 short June to 5743th and 216 58th Bde. Received 1000 goggles Antigas, 1000 prs gloves Fingerless.	NS
			90 Green Breech and 15 Pistol Signal 1"	NS
	4th		Received 52 mincing machines	NS
	5th		Received 4 horse clipping machines and 104 Grenades Dummy	NS
	7th		Received 13,000 pair of Mittens	NS
	8th		Received 16,500 pair Gloves Worsted and 2000 prs Goggles Antigas	NS
	9th		Received 598 pair of Gum Boots	NS
	10th		Received for H.Q. Coy A.S.C. 3 Wagons G.S.3, 2 Wagons Sunderland etc. Received 50 Units S.L., 100 Pt Boots Fs	NS
			and 448 Prs Gum Boots Thigh. Returned 1 gun 18 pr. for D Battery 86th Bde to replace 1 with Bulged Bore.	NS
	14th		Received 1 gun 16 pr for D Battery 86th Bde R.F.A.	NS
	15th		D.D.O.13 Army indited the Depot. Received 104 Ammt. revolver unit 23 Bangalore.	NS
	17th		Received 12 Rifles with Telescopic Sights, 1055 Grenade Carriers, unit 4 Handcarts.	NS
	18th		Received 1045 Tops and 1055 Wrenches for Short Cap, 400 Sanitary Tent Folding, 1 Bath + 2 Heaters for Baths	NS
	19th		Received 15 Compasses Magnetic Plane Table.	NS

Army Form C. 2118

WAR DIARY
or
INTELLIGENCE SUMMARY
(Erase heading not required.)

Instructions regarding War Diaries and Intelligence Summaries are contained in F.S. Regs., Part II. and the Staff Manual respectively. Title Pages will be prepared in manuscript.

Place	Date May 1915	Hour	Summary of Events and Information	Remarks and references to Appendices
	24.		Received 50 Steel Helmets, 210 Sling Stretcher and 361 Glones Huyerlin	105
	21.		Received 1 Vickers Machine gun for N°15 M.M. Gun Battery	105
	22.		Received 11 Bicycles	105
	23.		Moved to Loover Huilo	105
	28.		Received 15 Wagon limbered lp for Rivt Train, also 35 Magazines for Lewis M Guns.	105
	29.		Received 10 Carriages Ambulance Stretcher	105
	30.		Received 200 Steel Helmets, also 3 Web for Snipers	105

W. Smith Captain
DADOS 14th Division

Dec 1915

CONFIDENTIAL

WAR DIARY
OF
D.A.D.O.S. 19TH DIVISION
FROM 1st TO 31st DECEMBER 1915

WAR DIARY
or
INTELLIGENCE SUMMARY

(Erase heading not required.)

Army Form C. 2118

Instructions regarding War Diaries and Intelligence Summaries are contained in F. S. Regs., Part II. and the Staff Manual respectively. Title Pages will be prepared in manuscript.

Place	Date Feb 1915	Hour	Summary of Events and Information	Remarks and references to Appendices
	2nd		Received 12 Machines Horse Clipping. Returned 194 Goats Sheepskin to Base	WS
	3rd		Received 200 pairs of Socks Lumbermen's	WS
	4th		Received 116 Clamps Carrying Body, 48 Oval Adjusting Clamps, and 116 Straps Chitral Spindle	WS
	5th		Moved to Berun. Received 110 Rifles Very	WS
	10th		Received 1250 pairs of Gum Boots from 11th Corps	WS
	11th		Received 270 Steel Helmets, also 765 Gumboots thigh from 11th Corps	WS
	12th		Received 52 Bags for Carriage of Machine Gun	WS
	13th		Received 6 Periscopes No.14 from 11th Corps	WS
	14th		Received 16,390 Lebel Pattern Smoke Helmets	WS
	16th		Received 3000 pr Puttees and 150 pr Trousers for Reserve, also 11 Machine Horse Clipping + 12 Bicycles	WS
	17th		Received 6 Anemometers, 14 Compasses Trimmetric and 150 Steel Helmets	WS
	22nd		Received 2 Boxes Small Ammunition Filled	WS
	23rd		Received 200 Braziers	WS
	24th		Received 1350 prs Trousers for Reserve	WS
	25th		Received 2000 Mufflers	WS
	26th		Received 1 Goods Cart for "C" Battery 86th Bde R.F.A., 50 Steel Helmets and 1750 Balaclavas	WS
	27th		Received 110 Rugs Dummy Figures	WS
	28th		Received 5 Braziers, 9 Rifles with Martini Sights and 1 Bivouac Tent	WS
	29th		Received 8 Handcarts for 67 T.M. Battery and 1 Water Cart for 5th S. Wales Borderers	WS
	30th		Received 200 Braziers and 1000 pairs of Soles Inner	WS

W Smith Captain
D.A.D.O.S. 19th Division

CONFIDENTIAL WAR DIARY OF DADOS 19th DIVISION FROM 1st TO 31st JANUARY 1916.

Army Form C. 2118

WAR DIARY
or
INTELLIGENCE SUMMARY
(Erase heading not required.)

Instructions regarding War Diaries and Intelligence Summaries are contained in F.S. Regs., Part II. and the Staff Manual respectively. Title Pages will be prepared in manuscript.

Place	Date Jan 1916	Hour	Summary of Events and Information	Remarks and references to Appendices
	2nd		Received 33 Seats of authenticals	WS
	3rd		Received 5250 Leather fortinages to Steel Helmets, also 5105 pistoris for Rivl Reserve	WS
	4th		Received 240 Dungaree Suits	WS
	6th		Purchased 6 Sewing Machines for Brigade Tailors Shops	WS
	7th		Received 150 Greaves S.D. to complete Divisional Reserve	WS
	9th		Received 124 Rules Washing 3½ galls for Billets	WS
	11th		Received 10 Steel Helmets and 102 Reps Burning Spraillers	WS
	13th		Purchased 9 Pails of Axeltone and 46 Hair Cutting Machines	WS
	14th		Received from 1st Corps 117 P.S. Boots £.S, 13 Pr Gum Boots Short, and 259 P.S. Gum Boots Thigh	WS
	16th		Received 100 Steel Helmets	WS
	17th		Instruction in repair of Gum Boots arrived	WS
	18th		Lieut: S.A.W. Arnier A.D.D. joined for instruction under DADOS	WS
	19th		Received 14 Bicycles, 100 Steel Helmets and 39 Electric Torches	WS
	20th		Instructor in repair of Gum Boots left to join Guards Divn. Received 12 Periscopes No. 9 for Field Coys RE	WS
	22nd		Received 360 Spl. Sulsa Minute Helmets, 17 Steel Helmets and 100 Veils for Snipers, A.D.O.S. 10th Corps visited Depôt	WS
	23rd		Moved to Verenville. Received 6 Asturan ACs and 80 Cartridges for Verey ALS.	WS
	25th		Lieut Wording A.D.D. Bart expert arrived. Received 500 prs of P.S. Boots, and 100 prs Gum Boots Short.	WS
	26th		Lieut Wording ADD left for Guards Division. Received One H.5" Howr for "D" Battery 83rd Bde RFA	WS
	28th		Received 1 G.S. Wagon for 86th Bde. Divnl, 1 Cart Maximer for "D" Battery 83rd Bde RFA, 500 "P" Sulsa Patts Helmets for Divl Reserve, 15 Bicycles, 9 Handlespade grips for Seven M. guns, and 50 Steel Helmets	WS

1875 Wt. W593/826 1,000,000 4/15 J.B.C. & A. A.D.S.S./Forms/C. 2118.

Army Form C. 2118

WAR DIARY
or
INTELLIGENCE SUMMARY

(Erase heading not required.)

Instructions regarding War Diaries and Intelligence Summaries are contained in F. S. Regs., Part II. and the Staff Manual respectively. Title Pages will be prepared in manuscript.

Place	Date	Hour	Summary of Events and Information	Remarks and references to Appendices
	29th Jan 1916		Received 106 Trench Artillure	WS
	31st		Received 50 Vermorel Sprayers	WS
	31-1-16			

W Smith Captain
D.A.D.O.S. 19th Division

CONFIDENTIAL

WAR DIARY

OF

DADOS 19th DIVISION

FROM 1st TO 29th FEBRUARY

1916.

D.A.D.O.S. 19th Div. Vol. 7

WAR DIARY
or
INTELLIGENCE SUMMARY

Army Form C. 2118

(Erase heading not required.)

Place	Date	Hour	Summary of Events and Information	Remarks and references to Appendices
	April 1916 3rd		Capt. W. Smith A.D.D. left for 51st Division. Lieut. E. Austiwen R.O.D. assumed the duties of D.A.D.O.S. 19th Division	[illeg]
	5th		Received 300 Steel Helmets and 523 Handle loading Magazine Lewis guns	[illeg]
	8th		Received 200 Steel Helmets	[illeg]
	11th		Received 500 Steel Helmets, 3 Rifles with telescopic sights, and 16 sets of Harness	[illeg]
	15th		Received 100 Steel Helmets	[illeg]
	17th		Proceeded to G.H.Q. for Helmets. Received 100 Steel Helmets sent over from Grands Rivr. No 9 Food Carriers, 8 Handles	[illeg]
	19th		322 Verminal Sprayers, 20 Sabrine Kits, & 2 French Washers.	[illeg]
	20th		N°. 06122 [illeg] A/Lieut. A. Stanley R.O.E. joined for instruction in duties of A.D.O.S. W.D.	[illeg]
	21st		Received 134 Pas. Gunwheels short, 200 Bulls Watching, and 750 Steel Helmets	[illeg]
	22nd		Received 300 Rivets to Latrine	[illeg]
	23rd		Received 200 Steel Helmets, 36 Cartridges Saluredes to Washing lights, and 22 Runner lights	[illeg]
	25th		Received 14. 1000 R.H. Gas Helmets, 200 Steel Helmets, and 275 Pt. H. S. Rods	[illeg]
	27th		Received 100 Steel Helmets	[illeg]
	29th		Received 1 G.S. Wagon	[illeg]
			Received 1 W.D. 7 Diae lights	[illeg]

Lauriston Nunn
Lieut
D.A.D.O.S. 19th Div

CONFIDENTIAL

War Diary

OF

DADOS 19th Division

From 1st To 31st March 1916

Army Form C. 2118

WAR DIARY
or
INTELLIGENCE SUMMARY
(Erase heading not required.)

Instructions regarding War Diaries and Intelligence Summaries are contained in F. S. Regs., Part II. and the Staff Manual respectively. Title Pages will be prepared in manuscript.

Place	Date	Hour	Summary of Events and Information	Remarks and references to Appendices
	March 1916			
	1st		Received 2 Vickers gun for No 13. M.M. gun Battery and 200 Steel Helmets	
	2nd		Received 2 Stromber horns	
	3rd		Lieut L.H. Williams A.O.D. joined for duty	
	4th		Received 6 Handcarts for T.M. Battys, and 1 Aliposcee	
	5th		Received 168 Box Pattern Respirators	
	6th		Lieut L.A.W. Stoner left to join 35th Division. Received 3 Handcarts for T.M. Battys	
	7th		Received 200 Steel Helmets and 1 Wagon Lift Spring R.E.	
	8th		Received 100 Steel Helmets, also 2 Handcarts for T.M. Batty	
	9th		Received 76 Knobkerries	
	10th		Received 1 Handcart for T.M. Batty, 150 Steel Helmets, 15 Knobkerries, and 96 Box Respirators	
	11th		Received 100 Steel Helmets	
	13th		Received 6 mounting field service jars, and 2 Rifle Batteries	
	14th		Received 400 Steel Helmets	
	15th		Received 6 dispensers for service jars, and 1 Vickers gun for 578th M.G. Company	
	16th		Received 50 Box Respirators and 21 battery gun sights	
	17th		Received Vickers gun for 576 & M.G. Company	
	19th		Received 33 mounting field service, 39 Box Respirators, and 1 service gun for 10th Worcester Regt	
	20th		Received 12 mounting dispensers for Vickers gun, and 13, 6th R.H. Amore Helmets	
	21st		Received 1 service gun for 6th Worcester Regt, and 115 PH H.S. Armois	
	22nd		Received 600 Steel Helmets, 6 mounting Tripods, and 1 service gun for 10th Worcester Regt	

Army Form C. 2118

WAR DIARY
or
INTELLIGENCE SUMMARY

(Erase heading not required.)

Instructions regarding War Diaries and Intelligence Summaries are contained in F. S. Regs., Part II. and the Staff Manual respectively. Title Pages will be prepared in manuscript.

Place	Date March 1916	Hour	Summary of Events and Information	Remarks and references to Appendices
	23rd		Received 150 Steel Helmets, 5140 P.H. Amore Helmets, and 84 Box Pattern Respiration	
	24th		Received 300 Steel Helmets, and 1 Service jerkin for 1st Worcester Regt	
	25th		Received 242 Boxes Belt Ammunition .303	
	26th		Received 44 Box Pattern Respirators, 50 Prs Boots Ankle German Pattern	
	29th		Received 500 Steel Helmets	
	30th		Received 6 Rifle Batteries and 145 Box Pattern Respirators	
	31st		Received 4 Vickers Trench M Guns, and 1 Wagon G.S. for 19th Divl Train	

31.3.16.

Lieut:
D.A.D.O.S. 19th Division

DADOS
19 D
Vol 9

CONFIDENTIAL

WAR DIARY

OF

D.A.D.O.S. 19th Division

FROM 1st TO 30th APRIL

1916

WAR DIARY
or
INTELLIGENCE SUMMARY

(Erase heading not required.)

Army Form C. 2118

Instructions regarding War Diaries and Intelligence Summaries are contained in F.S. Regs., Part II. and the Staff Manual respectively. Title Pages will be prepared in manuscript.

Place	Date	Hour	Summary of Events and Information	Remarks and references to Appendices
	April 1916			
	1st		Received 75 Rifle Racks, 2 Lewis gun Wrappers, 3 Supercopes for Lewis guns, 3 Rests for firing Rifle Grenades and 30 Shields for protection of Bombers	
	2nd		Received 300 Steel Helmets and 11 Food Containers	
	3rd		Received 17 Battery Gun Sights	
	6th		Received 750 Steel Helmets, 2 Lamps Electric Aiming and 24 Box Respirators	
	7th		Received 1 Vickers-Maxim Machine gun mounting	
	10th		Received 550 Steel Helmets	
	11th		Received 1 Water Cart for 193 D.A.C., 28 Battery Gun Sights and 12 Posts Aiming Electric	
	15th		Moved to Murillee. Received 1000 Steel Helmets	
	19th		Moved to Warnimont Farries	
	20th		Received 6 Cases of Sound Instruments and 8 Handcarts for Trench Mortar Batteries	
	22nd		Received 3,990 P.H. Smoke Helmets for Reserve	
	23rd		Received 15,010 " " " " " " " "	
	24th		Received 500 Steel Helmets	
	27th		Received 1000 Steel Helmets	
	29th		Received 950 Steel Helmets	
	3oth		Received 4 Handcarts for Trench Mortar Batteries	

J.M.Williams
Captain
DADOS 11th Div
1-5-1916.

DADOS 19th DW VOL 10

CONFIDENTIAL

WAR DIARY OF D.A.D.O.S. 19th DIVISION.

FROM 1st TO 31st MAY 1916.

WAR DIARY
or
INTELLIGENCE SUMMARY
(Erase heading not required.)

Army Form C. 2118

Place	Date	Hour	Summary of Events and Information	Remarks and references to Appendices
	May 1916			
	1st		Received 35 Vacuum Bulbs, and 1 Lewis gun for 8th Worcester Regt.	
	3rd		Received 4 Handcarts for Trench Mortar Batteries	
	4th		Received 1 Maxim gun for 5 & 8 7th Machine gun Coy	
	6th		Received 1 Vickers gun and 4 Stokes mortars	
	7th		Moved 15 4 Wheelers	
	9th		Received 100 Vermorel Sprayers	
	10th		700 Anti gas goggles received for Divisional Reserve	
	11th		Received 30 C.S.L. and 180 Willox Tents	
	13th		Received 52 Lewis Guns	
	15th		Received 1 Lewis gun for 5th S. Wales Bord.; 150 Stretcher Mules; 300 Cases Picalanne, and 200 Cases Rodea	
	16th		Received 1 Lewis gun for 9th Welch Regt. and 1950 Bucket Pattern Bomb Carriers	
	18th		Received 70 C.S.L. Tents	
	19th		Received 25 C.S.L. Tents	
	25th		Received 2 Vickers guns in exchange for 2 Maxims, 2705 Steel Helmets, 832 Watch Wires, 1 Vermorel Sprayer, 18 Box Respirators, 7 C.S.L Tents and 1 Marquee	
	26th		Received 50 Ayrton Stoves, 168 Box Respirators and 650 Carriers grenade Waistcoat River.	
	27th		Received 50 C.S.L Tents, in Page tool Accessories Field and 3 Periscopes No 14.	
	28th		Received 5D C.S.L Tents, 416 Rifles Rifle No 7, 132 Box Respirations, 650 Bull Bag grenade carriers	
	30th		Received 94 Box Respirators	
	31st		Received 1000 P.H.g. Anomre Helmets	

Captain
D.A.D.V.S., 19th Division

CONFIDENTIAL

WAR DIARY
OF
DADOS 19th DIVISION
FROM 1st TO 30th JUNE
1916

Army Form C. 2118

WAR DIARY
or
INTELLIGENCE SUMMARY
(Erase heading not required.)

Instructions regarding War Diaries and Intelligence Summaries are contained in F.S. Regs., Part II. and the Staff Manual respectively. Title Pages will be prepared in manuscript.

Place	Date June 1916	Hour	Summary of Events and Information	Remarks and references to Appendices
	1st		Received 400 Steel Helmets	
	2nd		Received 5 m Steel Helmets and 25 Handcarts for Trench Mortar Batteries	
	7th		Received 1 - 18 pounder QF gun for "C" Batty 86B Bde R.F.A.	
	10th		Received 5 m Smoke Carrier Baskets and 1484 - 2 pocket	
	15th		Received 300 Steel Helmets	
	16th		Received 700 Magazines for Lewis Guns. Moved to Frechencourt	
	17th		Received 10 Handcarts for B.Coy 15th Bde	
	21st		Received 10 - " - " - and 12 French Signalling Lamps	
	22nd		Received 354 Magazines for Lewis Guns and 10 Handcarts	
	23rd		Received 500 Steel Helmets, 2 Periscopes No 14, 250 Waterbags & 3 French Signalling Lamps	
	24th		Received 900 Magazines for Lewis Guns	
	25th		Received 250 Waddings and 73 Sheep Jackets	
	26th		Received 200 Magazines for Lewis Guns, 4 Handcarts, and Wheelie Cart for D.A.M.S Col.	
	27th		Received 12 Vermoral Sprayers	
	29th		Moved to Buire	

Captain
DADOS 19th Division

CONFIDENTIAL.

WAR DIARY

of

D.A.D.O.S. 19th DIVISION.

FROM 1st TO 31st JULY, 1916.

WAR DIARY
or
INTELLIGENCE SUMMARY

(Erase heading not required.)

Army Form C. 2118

Instructions regarding War Diaries and Intelligence Summaries are contained in F. S. Regs., Part II. and the Staff Manual respectively. Title Pages will be prepared in manuscript.

Place	Date	Hour	Summary of Events and Information	Remarks and references to Appendices
	July 1916			
	1st		Received 35 Handcarts for Lewis guns, 4 Hyperscopes for Lewis guns and 316 Box Respirators	
	3rd		Received 142 Box Respirators and 172 Wild sprayers for Lewis guns	
	5th		Received 1 No 7 Rifle Sight	
	6th		Received 4 Lewis guns for 22nd Durham L.I.	
	7th		Received 1728 Carriers Magazine Covers, 103 Box Respirators, 37 Handcarts for Lewis guns & 1000 Steel Helmets	
	9th		Received 3 Lewis guns for 8th Gloucester Regt and 3 for 8th N. Staffs Regt	
	10th		Received 2 Lewis guns for 6th Welsh Regt	
	11th		Received 1 - 4.5" Howitzer and 1 No 7 Rifle Sight for D/86 R.F.A.	
	13th		Received 150 Steel Helmets	
	14th		Received 1 - 4.5" Howitzer Carriage for D/86 T.F.A., 2 Vickers guns for 563 M.G. Coy & 200 Steel Helmets	
	18th		Received 4500 Steel Helmets, 20 Steel Swivels	
	19th		Received 696 Magazines Lewis guns	
	21st		Received 5 B.D. Saddle Helmets	
	22nd		Received 5 B.D. Steel Helmets	
	25th		Received 30 Handcarts for Lewis guns	
	26th		Received 3 B.D. Ear Drum Protectors, 27 Handcarts for Lewis guns, 4 Rifles Signal "L" for Lieut Burton and 1 G.S. Wagon for 19th D.A.C.	
	27th		Received 4 D Bicycles, 1 Vickers gun for 575 M.G. Coy, 150 Steel Helmets and 34 Machine gun Belts	
	28th		Received 1 Lewis gun for 15th G.C. Hunts Regt	
	29th		D.D. D.S. 1st Army Inspected Depot	
	30th		Received 4 Swivel Pattern Dynamite Scales, 1 Watercart for 4th Cheshire Regt, and 1 G.S. Wagon for the 19th D.A.C.	
	31st		Received 4 Lewis gun Handcarts, 1 No 14 Periscope and 6 No 5 Periscopes	

J. McElhenney
Captain
D.A.D.O.S. 19th Divn

19/DADOS/13

CONFIDENTIAL WAR DIARY OF DADOS 19TH DIVISION.

FROM 1st TO 31st AUGUST 1916.

Army Form C. 2118

WAR DIARY
or
INTELLIGENCE SUMMARY
(Erase heading not required.)

Instructions regarding War Diaries and Intelligence Summaries are contained in F. S. Regs., Part II. and the Staff Manual respectively. Title Pages will be prepared in manuscript.

Place	Date	Hour	Summary of Events and Information	Remarks and references to Appendices
	August 1916			
	2nd		Received 500 Steel Helmets and 22 Hygroscopes for Lewis gun	
	5th		Moved to Bailleul. Received 1 Lewis gun for 93rd RFA Welsh How. and 4 Periscopes No. 14	
	9th		Received 5912 P.H.G. Helmets	
	10th		Received 10,350 P.H.G. Helmets	
	11th		Moved to Westoutre	
	12th		Lieut. H.C. Carlile A.D.D. arrived from O.Y. for instruction in duties of D.A.D.V.S.	
	13th		Received 1 Lewis gun for 78th E Lancs Regt.	
	14th		Received 10 Handcarts for Trench Mortar Batteries	
	15th		Received 1 G/S wagon for D.A. Coln. and 1 for Divnl Train	
	16th		Received 18 Dummy Heads and 40 Luminous Aiming Posts	
	21st		Received 500 Steel Helmets	
	22nd		Received 400 Steel Helmets	
	23rd		Received 1 Lewis gun for 10th R.E. Warwick Regt.	
	24th		Received 1 Ammn Wagon and Limber for "B" Battery 88th 174th RFA	
	25th			
	26th		Received 517 Lewis gun magazines	
	31st		Moved to Locre. Received 700 Steel Helmets.	

[signature]
Captain
D.A.D.V.S. 19th Division

CONFIDENTIAL

War Diary

OF

D.A.D.O.S. 19th Division.

From 1st To 30th September.

1916.

WAR DIARY
or
INTELLIGENCE SUMMARY

(Erase heading not required.)

Army Form C. 2118

Place	Date	Hour	Summary of Events and Information	Remarks and references to Appendices
	April 1918			
	5th		Received 10000 Small Box Respirators	
	6th		Moved to Bailleul	
	9th		Received 1000 Small Box Respirators + 1 Lewis gun from 8th Warwick Regt	
	10th		Received 10000 Small Box Respirators	
	13th		Received 1000 Small Box Respirators + 26 Ayrepenere for Lewis Guns	
	15th		Received 24 Rifle Rnds Inoveners 31 Rifle Pointers Elevating	
	18th		Received 10000 Small Box Respirators	
	20th		Moved to Merris. Lieut: H.C. Carlisle A.D.D. left the Division. Received Service Rifle Sight for 9.45 inch Trench mortar	
	24th		Received 2 Hutchkiss Machine Guns	
	25th		Received 16 Prismoscoves for Medical Officer use	
	27th		Received 3,200 Small Box Respirators with 2,950 Steel Helmets	
	29th		Received 3400 Small Box Respirators and 1 Kickers Gun for 5th Machine Gun Coy	
	30th		Received 26 Lewis Guns.	

CONFIDENTIAL
WAR DIARY
OF
DADOS 19th DIVISION

FROM 1st TO 31st OCTOBER.

1916

Army Form C. 2118

WAR DIARY
or
INTELLIGENCE SUMMARY
(Erase heading not required.)

Instructions regarding War Diaries and Intelligence Summaries are contained in F.S. Regs., Part II. and the Staff Manual respectively. Title Pages will be prepared in manuscript.

Place	Date October 1916	Hour	Summary of Events and Information	Remarks and references to Appendices
	2nd		Received 196D Box Respirators	
	5th		Moved to Mariencourt	
	6th		Moved to Authie	
	10th		Received two 4".5" Amm: Carriages for D/67	
	11th		Received 160 Box Respirators	
	13th		Received 832 Magazines 9mm Jun, and 700 Hawken loading magazines	
	15th		Received 1 Lewis Gun for 7th Rif. & Lancaster Reg.	
	19th		Moved to Warley, Received 1222 Steel Helmets, and 267D Pr Boots F.S.	
	22nd		Received 950 Steel Helmets	
	24th		Received 480 Pr. Boots F.S.	
	25th		Received one 18 pdr Gun and one Carriage for A/87 RFA	
	26th		Received one 18 pdr Gun for A/112 RFA	
	30th		Received 130 Sets of Panabadlery and 176 Revolvers in exchange for Spanish Pattern	
	31st		Received 11 Food Containers	

31-10-1916

Signature
Captain
D.A.D.O.S. 19th Division

Vol 16

CONFIDENTIAL
WAR DIARY
OF
D.A.D.O.S. 19ᵗʰ DIVISION.
FROM 1ˢᵗ TO 30ᵗʰ NOVEMBER.
1916.

WAR DIARY
or
INTELLIGENCE SUMMARY

Army Form C. 2118

(Erase heading not required.)

Date	Hour	Summary of Events and Information	Remarks and references to Appendices
Nov 1916 1st		Received 1 Limber GS 15 pr Wagon for A/113 RFA	
2nd		Received 1 Wagon G/S for 19th DAC and 1 Watercart for A/113 RFA	
4th		Received one 18 pr Gun for A/112 RFA.	
5th		Received Vickers gun for 56th MG Coy and 1 for 57th MG Coy, 1 GS Wagon for 19th DAC	
8th		Received 18 Pr Watch Signal 1 inch for MG Coys	
11th		Received one 18 pr Gun and Carriage for A/113 RFA	
12th		Received 2 Bruno gun for 7th E Lancs and 1 for 4th Welsh Regt, 1 Watercart for B/113 RFA	
13th		Received one 4.5" Howitzer for D/68 RFA	
14th		Received one 18 pr Gun Carriage for C/112 RFA and one for A/113 RFA, Bruno Gun for 7th L.N.Lancs Regt.	
15th		Received one 18 pr Gun for C/111 RFA, and 1 GS Wagon for H&S Coy 25th Dv Train	
16th		Received one 4.5" Howz and Carriage for D/112 RFA and 1 GS Wagon for 35th D.A.C	
17th		Received one 18 pr Gun Carriage for C/110 RFA	
19th		Received 3 Vickers gun for 56th M.G. Coy	
21st		Received one 18 pr gun for C/110 RFA.	
22nd		Received one 18 pr gun + Carriage for C/111 RFA, and one 18 pr Carriage each for B/87 and A/112 RFA	
25th		Moved to Bernaville	
29th		Received 1 Bruno gun for 1st N.Staffs Regt	
30th		Received 5 Bruno gun for 8th N Staffs Regt.	

30-11-1916

CONFIDENTIAL
WAR DIARY
OF
D.A.D.O.S. 19TH DIVISION
FROM 1ST TO 31ST DECEMBER.
1916.

WAR DIARY
or
INTELLIGENCE SUMMARY

(Erase heading not required.)

Army Form C. 2118

Place	Date	Hour	Summary of Events and Information	Remarks and references to Appendices
	1st		Received 21,000 Repairs and Record Outfits for Small Box Respirators	
	3rd		Received 2 Vickers Guns for 57th Machine Gun Corps.	
	4th		Received 1 Vickers Gun for 58th Machine Gun Coy.	
	5th		Received 1 Lewis Gun for 10th Royal Warwick Regt.	
	7th		Received 3 Lewis Guns for 8th Gloucester Regt.	
	8th		Received 24 Lewis Guns, 12 Battalions of Infantry @ 2 each.	
	14th		Received 12 Hyposcopes Lewis Gun.	
	20th		Received 17,380 discs Sanctify by Eqn.	
	21st		Received 16 carriages G.S. 4"5" How: for 2/1/6 R.F.A.	
	24th		Received 13,000 Cartridges S.A. Dummy Drill .303"	
	26th		Received 3A + chargers regarding collapsible, and 1 wagon G.S. for HSAC.	
	27th		Received 6,240 Box Respirators Small.	

J M Cherry
Captain
D.A.D.O.S. 19th Division

Vol 18

CONFIDENTIAL.

WAR DIARY

OF

D.A.D.O.S. 19th DIVISION.

FROM 1st TO 31st JANUARY

1917.

Army Form C. 2118

WAR DIARY
or
INTELLIGENCE SUMMARY

(Erase heading not required.)

Instructions regarding War Diaries and Intelligence Summaries are contained in F.S. Regs., Part II. and the Staff Manual respectively. Title Pages will be prepared in manuscript.

Place	Date	Hour	Summary of Events and Information	Remarks and references to Appendices
	January 1917			
	1st		Received 20 Handcarts for Trench Mortars & 9350 Box Respirators Issued	
	2nd		Received two 2" Trench Mortars for X.19 T.M. Battery and two for Z.19 T.M. Battery	
	10th		Moved to Corun	
	14th		Received 1 mnt T Bucker Wagon for A/87 R.F.A. and 1 for B/87 R.F.A.	
	15th		Received 1-18 pr Gun Carriage for A/86 R.F.A., 1 Watercart for A/87 R.F.A. & 10 Handcarts for Trenchwork	
	17th		Received 1 G.S. wagon for 5th A. Horse, 50 Steel Helmets With Visors, + H Anti-Aircraft M.G. Mountings	
	20th		Received 20 hot Food Containers	
	21st		Received 20 hot Food Containers	

[signature]
Captain
DADOS 19th Division
31-1-17

CONFIDENTIAL.

WAR DIARY.
OF
D.A.D.O.S. 19th DIVISION.

FROM 1st TO 28th FEBRUARY.
1917.

Army Form C. 2118

WAR DIARY
or
INTELLIGENCE SUMMARY

(Erase heading not required.)

Instructions regarding War Diaries and Intelligence Summaries are contained in F.S. Regs., Part II. and the Staff Manual respectively. Title Pages will be prepared in manuscript.

Place	Date Feb 1917	Hour	Summary of Events and Information	Remarks and references to Appendices
	2nd		Received 24 Lewis guns.	
	5th		Received 1 Carriage B/F 18 pdr for B/86 RFA and 1 Wagon Limber for 9th R.F. Wash turn	
	8th		Received 4 Camel Gun wheel supports for trial	
	9th		Received 1950 Steel Helmets fitted with Chain Curtains	
	10th		Received 1 - 3" Stokes mortar for 57th Trench mortar Battery	
	11th			
	12th		Received 6 Rule sets for sight trench mortar Batteries, + 12 Hygrometers for Lewis guns	
	13th		Received 3 - 18 pdr B.L. Carriages, 1 for C/87 and 2 for A/87 R.F.A	
	14th		Received 1 - 4.5" Howitzer for D/87 and 1 - 18 pdr B/F for C/155 R.F.A	
	21st		Received 1 Watercart for C/87 and 1 for B/68 R.F.A.	
	23rd		Received 1 - 18 pdr gun for C/86 and 1 for A/87 R.F.A. 646 rifles ammunition	

Captain
D.A.D.O.S. 19th Division

CONFIDENTIAL

WAR DIARY

OF

D.A.D.O.S. 19TH DIVISION.

FROM 1ST TO 31ST MARCH.

1917.

WAR DIARY
or
INTELLIGENCE SUMMARY
(Erase heading not required.)

Army Form C. 2118

Instructions regarding War Diaries and Intelligence Summaries are contained in F. S. Regs., Part II. and the Staff Manual respectively. Title Pages will be prepared in manuscript.

Place	Date	Hour	Summary of Events and Information	Remarks and references to Appendices
	March 1917			
	1st		Received 1 – 4'5" Howitzer for D/67 C⁄y R.F.A. and 1 Watercart for 9th Cheshire Regt.	
	4th		Moved to Brw. Received 12 "P" Grenade Carriers	
	5th		Received 1–18 par gun for B/155 CXY R.F.A. and 38 horses signalling French Pattern	
	7th		Received 1 H/W d/r for 98 DAC, 1 Watercart each for B/155 R.F.A. and 1/9th Lancaster Regt., 1 Motor Car each for B/66 and B/155 R.F.A.	
	10th		Moved to Beauquesne	
	12th		Moved to Warnimont Wood	
	16th		Moved to Miraumont	
	20th		Moved to Flêtre. Received 24 Lewis Guns. 1 Watercart each for A/87, B/87 and 88th Howitzer Bty.	
	31st		1 Motor Car for 9th Welch Regt., 1 Wagon M.T. for 149 DAC, and Proceeding Kitchen to 8th N. Staff Regt. Moved to Watountre	

Captain
DADOS 1st[?] Div.
31–8–1917

CONFIDENTIAL

WAR DIARY

OF

D.A.D.O.S 19TH DIVISION

FROM 1ST TO 30TH APRIL, 1917.

WAR DIARY
or
INTELLIGENCE SUMMARY
(Erase heading not required.)

Army Form C. 2118

Instructions regarding War Diaries and Intelligence Summaries are contained in F.S. Regs., Part II. and the Staff Manual respectively. Title Pages will be prepared in manuscript.

Place	Date	Hour	Summary of Events and Information	Remarks and references to Appendices
	April 1917			
	2nd		Received 1 Maltese Cart for 7th R.N. Lancs Regt, 1 Watercart for 6th N. Staffs Regt, 1 Wagon Limbered G.S. for 1st DAC and 1 Pettey Kitchen Travelling for 5th S. Wales Borderers	
	4th		Received 1 - 4.5" Howitzer for D/67 R.F.A. and 1 Hind portion of Wagon Limbered G.S. for 1/8th R. Warwick Regt	
	7th		Received 2 - 3" Stokes Mortars for Divisional School	
	9th		Received 1 W/cart for 1/4th Signal Coy R.E.	
	11th		Received 1 Watercart for 7/6 Gwrs Regt and 1 for 1/8th T. mim. and 1 Body/Kitchen Travelling 7 Ethus R	
	20th		Received 9/6 No II Barrels Vickers gun and 2HD and II Liner Miroye attachment	
	22nd		Received 1 h/s wagon for 250th Tunnelling Coy R.E.	
	25th		Received 1 - 3" Stokes Mortar for 5th T.M. Battery and 16 Dannet Priwrover for Rivle	
	27th		Received 1 Watercart for D/68 R.F.A. and 1 for 1/8th R. Warwick Regt	

Captain
D.A.D.O.S. 1st Division
30-4-17.

CONFIDENTIAL
WAR DIARY
OF
D.A.D.O.S. 19TH DIVISION.
FROM 1ST TO 31ST MAY
1917.

Army Form "C. 2118

WAR DIARY
or
INTELLIGENCE SUMMARY
(Erase heading not required.)

Instructions regarding War Diaries and Intelligence Summaries are contained in F. S. Regs., Part II. and the Staff Manual respectively. Title Pages will be prepared in manuscript.

Place	Date	Hour	Summary of Events and Information	Remarks and references to Appendices
	May 1917			
	3rd		Moved to hut near Poperinghe. Received 1 Watercart for D¹ H⁴ 8ᵗʰ; 1 G.S. Wagon for DAC + 1 Mg hand G.S. limb for 1/5ᵗʰ Warwick Regt.	
	4ᵗʰ		Received 1 Vickers Gun for 56¹ M.G. Coy, 1 Watercart each for 5ᵗʰ Full Amsee, and A/86 RFA	
	6ᵗʰ		Received 10.6 ox extension for Smell Box Respirators	
	7ᵗʰ		Received 7.300 Extensions for Small Box Respirators, 1 Watercart each for 1/1ᵗʰ & Wilts Reg ₂ kitchens travelling Bodies each for 8/10ᵗʰ + 9/Welch Reg: + 1 Body Wagon limbered R.E. for 1/2 Signale Coy R.E.	
	11ᵗʰ		Moved to Westoutre.	
	13ᵗʰ		Received 6 N° 25 Respirators for M.G. Corpˢ + hind parts of Wagon limbered G.S. for 1/4 Welch Reg!	
	15ᵗʰ		Received 1 Watercart for 7/5 L.N. Lancs Regˢ, 7 Machines Chaff Cutting	
	16ᵗʰ		Received 1 Brain Gun for 1/5ᵗʰ RF Warwick Reg!	
	18ᵗʰ		Received 1 - 18 gun Gun and Carriage for B/58 TFA, 1 G.S. Wagon for DAC and 1 Bream Cart for 1/6 Cheshire Reg!	
	20ᵗʰ		Received 1 G.S. Wagon for 1/5ᵗʰ DAC + 2 hind parts of Wagons limbered G.S. for 5ᵗʰ S. Wales Bord:	
	23ʳᵈ		Received 2 Brain guns for 1/8 E. Lancs Reg; 2 G.S. Wagons for 1/4ᵗʰ DAC, 1 G.S. Wagon for 5ᵗʰ S. W. B., 1 fore part of Wagon limbered G.S. for each H.B. 5b and B/2ⁿᵈ 1/3 Lancaster Reg!, 1 Kitchen travelling body for 1/8ᵗʰ Warwick Reg!.	
	25ᵗʰ		Received 2 - 3" Stokes Munitions for 5/8ᵗʰ M.B. Battery	
	28ᵗʰ		Received 2 - 18 pʳ Carriages for C/87 RFA	
	29ᵗʰ		Received 1 Wagon limbered G.S. for 8¹/Cov R.E. 2 hind part Wagon limb GST 1 Body Kitchen travelling for 5ᵗʰ S.W.B", 1 Wagon limb G.S. for 1/4ᵗʰ DAC. 1 for 2/50ᵗʰ Tunnelling Coy R.E.	

[signatures]
DADOS 19ᵗʰ Divn 31-5-17

CONFIDENTIAL

WAR DIARY

OF

D.A.D.O.S 19ᵀᴴ DIVISION

FROM 1ˢᵀ TO 30ᵀᴴ JUNE

1917.

Army Form C. 2118

WAR DIARY
or
INTELLIGENCE SUMMARY
(Erase heading not required.)

Instructions regarding War Diaries and Intelligence Summaries are contained in F. S. Regs., Part II. and the Staff Manual respectively. Title Pages will be prepared in manuscript.

Place	Date	Hour	Summary of Events and Information	Remarks and references to Appendices
	June 1917			
	1st		Received 1 Watercart for 7th R.F. Lancaster Regt.	—
	4th		Received 1 Watercart for each 1/5 W.W. Regt, 5th M. Gun Coy + N°3 Section 19th D.A.C, 1 Wagon G/S and 1 Wagon Limbered Aust for 136 A.T. Coy R.E., 1 Wagon Pontoon for 81st yth Coy R.E, 1 Wag h/S Limbered for 9th R.E. Welsh + Fusiliers.	—
	6th		Received 1 Kitchen Travelling for 7th S. Lancs Regt.	—
	10th		Received 2 Lewis Gun for 1/5 Cheshire Regt, and 2 for 9th R.E. Welsh + Fusiliers	—
	11th		Received 2 Lewis Guns for 9th Welsh Regt.	—
	12th		Moved to Schernhendry.	—
	13th		Received 1 Wagon Amm'n 18 pdr for 13.88 R.F.A	—
	14th		Received 1 Lewis Gun for 7th E. Lancs Regt.	—
	15th		Received 1 Lewis Gun for 10th Worcester Regt.	—
	18th		Received 2 Vickers Guns for 5 Bn M.Gun Coy, 1 Wagon Limbered RE Body for 19th Signal Coy RE 1 Wagon G/S Limbered Finish for 5th M.Gun Coy, 1 Watercart for 13.87 R.F.A.	—
	20th		Moved to St. Jean Cappel	—
	28th		Received 1 G/S Wagon for N°2 Section 19th D.A.C.	—
	30th		Received 1 G/S Wagon for N°3 Section 19th D.A.C. + 1 Fore part Wag Limbered RE for 19 Signal Coy RE	—

V. E. Lambach
D A D O S 19th Division

CONFIDENTIAL.

WAR DIARY

OF

D.A.D.O.S. 19TH DIVISION.

FROM 1ST TO 31ST JULY

1917.

WAR DIARY
or
INTELLIGENCE SUMMARY

(Erase heading not required.)

Army Form C. 2118

Place	Date	Hour	Summary of Events and Information	Remarks and references to Appendices
	July 1917			
	2nd		Allowed to Leave. Received 1-18 pdr Gun for B/67 RFA	
	3rd		Received 1-18 pdr Gun for C/68 Bde RFA	
	10th		Received 1 Wagon Ammunition 18 pdr for A/57 RFA	
	12th		Received 1-18 pdr Gun for each A/57 and B/68 RFA, 1-18 pdr RFA, and 1-18 pdr Gun Carriage for C/67 RFA, and 1-18 pdr Gun Carriage for A/88 RFA	
	16		Received Vickers Gun for 57 M.G. Coy, and 1 G.S. Wagon for No 2 Section 19th D.A.C.	
	19th		Received 1 Lewis Gun for 8th Gloucester Regt.	
	24th		Received 1 Watercart for 8 2nd Lt. Coy R.E. + 1 Hind part of Wagon hindwheel G.S. for 9th Welch Regt.	
	26th		Received 2 Lewis Guns for 9th Welch Regt, 3 for 7th S. Lancs Regt, + 1 for 15th R.L Lancaster Regt.	
	28th		Received 1-3" Stokes Mortar for 56th T.M. Battery, Vickers Gun for 58 M.G. Coy + 1 Lewis Gun for 15th R.L Lancaster R	
	30th		Received 1 Vickers Gun for 57th Machine Gun Coy	
	31st		Received 1-3" Stokes Mortar for 58th T.M. Battery, 2-18 pdr Guns for C/67 RFA, and 1-18 pdr Gun for B/68 RFA.	

DADOS 19th Division
31-7-17

CONFIDENTIAL
WAR DIARY
OF
D.A.D.O.S 19ᵀᴴ DIVISION
FROM 1ˢᵀ TO 31ˢᵀ AUGUST
1917.

WAR DIARY
or
INTELLIGENCE SUMMARY
(Erase heading not required.)

Army Form C. 2118

Instructions regarding War Diaries and Intelligence Summaries are contained in F.S. Regs., Part II. and the Staff Manual respectively. Title Pages will be prepared in manuscript.

Place	Date Aug 1917	Hour	Summary of Events and Information	Remarks and references to Appendices
	1st		Received 1 G.S. Wagon for 3 Section 1st D.A.C., 1 Wagon G.S. R.E. for 19th Signal Coy R.E.; 1 Watercart for A. 67th R.F.A.	
	2nd		Received 2-16 pdr guns for B.87; 1 each for B.87, A.88, and B.88, and 10 April Amices for 57th Field Ambulance	
	3rd		Received 1 Wagon G/S for N°1 Section 19th D.A.C.	
	5th		Received 1 Limber Gun for 8th N.S.R. Regt.	
	7th		Moved to N° 1 Lewis Carrel	
	8th		Received 2 Wagons G/S for N°3 Section 19th D.A.C., and 1 for N°2 Coy, 19th Div. Train A.S.C.	
	10th		Moved to Lumbres	
	11th		Received 1 Wagon Ammns for C.87,B.88 R.F.A., 4 Vickers guns for 56 M.G. Coy, 3 for 58 M.G. Coy, 3 for 246th M.G. Coy, 4 Lewis guns for 7th E Lancs Regt, and 3 for 7th B Lancs Regt.	
	12th		Received 2 - 3" Stokes Mortars for 56 T.M. Battery; 1 Vickers gun for 58 M.G. Coy, and 3 Lewis guns for 7th L.N.L Regt.	
	13th		Received 8 Lewis guns for 7th R.L Lancs Regt, 3 for 7th L.N.L Regt, and 1 Wagon G/S for H 8 58 Inf Bde.	
	15th		Received 1 Wagon Ambulance G/S for 7th R.L Lancaster Regt.	
	18th		Received 1 Lewis gun for 7th L.N.L Regt.	
	23rd		Received 1 Wagon Limbered G/S for 5 G 7th Field Ambulance	
	29th		Moved to N° 1 Lewis Carrel	

CONFIDENTIAL

WAR DIARY

OF

D.A.D.O.S. 19th DIVISION

FROM 1st TO 30th SEPTEMBER

1917

WAR DIARY
or
INTELLIGENCE SUMMARY

Army Form C. 2118

(Erase heading not required.)

Instructions regarding War Diaries and Intelligence Summaries are contained in F.S. Regs., Part II. and the Staff Manual respectively. Title Pages will be prepared in manuscript.

Place	Date	Hour	Summary of Events and Information	Remarks and references to Appendices.
	Apr. 1917			
	3rd		Received 2 Lewis Guns for 1/4 E Lancs Regt + 1-3" Stokes Mortar for 57th T.M. Battery	
	8th		Received 1 Wagon Limbered W/S for H.Q. 57th Lnt T.M.B.	
	9th		Received 2 G.S. Wagons for 3 Section 10th D.A.C.	
	10th		Moved to Savy.	
	11th		Received 2 Lewis Guns for 6th Gloucester Regt.	
	18th		Received 1-18 pdn Gun + 1-16 Rn Carriage for A. 87 R.F.A.	
	19th		Received 1 Watercart for 7th S. Lancs Regt + 1 Vickers Gun for 56 M. Gun Coy	
	20th		Received 3 Vickers Guns for 56 M Gun Coy + 2 for 2n6 4th Gun Coy, 1 Lewis Gun for 1/4 R Lancaster Regt 1 Wagon Limb W/S Artil for 56 M.Gun Coy, 1 Wagon Limbered RE Books for 91st Coy RE + 1 complete Wagon Limbered W/S for 69th Coy RE	
	24th		Received 1-18 pdr Gun for C. 86 Bde R.F.A.	
	25th		Received 1-18 pdn Gun for C. 68 Bde R.F.A., 1 Wagon W/S for 3 Sec 10 DAC, 1 Body Wagon Limb RE for Inf Sig Regt	
	26th		Received 2 Lewis Guns for 6th Gloucester Regt, 3 for 9th Cheshire Regt, + 3 for 9th Welch Regt, 1 Vickers gun for 246 M Gun Coy, 1-18 pdn gun for C. 86 Bde R.F.A.	
	27th		Received 1-3" Stokes Mortar for 58th T.M. Battery	

Signed, Captain
D.A.D.O.S. 10th Division
30-9-17

CONFIDENTIAL
WAR DIARY
OF
D.A.D.O.S. 19th Division
FROM 1st TO 31st OCTOBER 1917

WAR DIARY
or
INTELLIGENCE SUMMARY
(Erase heading not required.)

Army Form C. 2118

Instructions regarding War Diaries and Intelligence Summaries are contained in F. S. Regs., Part II. and the Staff Manual respectively. Title Pages will be prepared in manuscript.

Place	Date	Hour	Summary of Events and Information	Remarks and references to Appendices
	Oct 1917			
	2nd		Received 1 Travelling Kitchen for 9th Gloucester Regt.	
	4th		Received 3 - 3" Stokes Mortars for 58th T.M. Battery	
	5th		Received 1 - 18 pdr gun for B.86 Bde R.F.A. and 1 Wagon Limbered W/S for 62nd Fd Coy R.E.	
	7th		Received 1 - 18 pdr gun for C.86 Bde R.F.A.	
	8th		Received 1 - 4.5" Howitzer Carriage for D.87 R.F.A. and 1 W/S Wagon for No 3 Sec. 19th D.A.C.	
	9th		Received 1 Lewis gun for 9th Cheshire Regt + 1 W/S Wagon for No 3 Section 19th D.A.C.	
	11th		Received 1 Lewis gun for 10th Welsh Regt + 1 for 9th R. Welsh Fusiliers	
	12th		Received 1 - 4.5" Howr for D.87 R.F.A. and 1 - 3" Stokes Mortar for 57th T.M. Battery	
	14th		Received 1 Lewis gun for 7th R. Lancaster Regt.	
	15th		Received 1 Wagon W/S for each 3 Sec + B Sec 19th D.A.C. + 1 Watercart for each B.87 R.F.A + 9th R. Welsh Fusiliers	
	17th		Received 1 Medicine Cart for H.86, 19th D.A.C. + 1 Wagon Limbd W/S Hind for 8th N. Staffs Regt	
	19th		Received 1 Vickers gun for 24th D. M.Gun Company	
	20th		Received 1 Lewis gun for 7th S. Lancs Regt.	
	25th		Received 1 - 4.5" Carriage for D.66 R.F.A., 1 Wagon limbered W/S for 69nd Fd Coy R.E. + 1 Pre rear Wag Limbd R.E. for 9th Coy R.E.	
	30th		Received 1 - 18 pdr Carriage for A.87 R.F.A., 1 Watercart for 9th Welsh Regt, 1 Wagon limbered W/S for 62nd Fd Coy R.E. + 1 Body Wagon limbd R.E. for 62nd Fd Coy R.E., 1 Pre rear Wagon limbd W/S for 62nd Sig. Coy R.E.	

CONFIDENTIAL

WAR DIARY

OF

D.A.D.O.S. 19TH DIVISION.

FROM 1st TO 30th NOVEMBER

1917.

Army Form C. 2118

WAR DIARY
or
INTELLIGENCE SUMMARY
(Erase heading not required.)

Instructions regarding War Diaries and Intelligence Summaries are contained in F.S. Regs., Part II. and the Staff Manual respectively. Title Pages will be prepared in manuscript.

Place	Date 1917	Hour	Summary of Events and Information	Remarks and references to Appendices
	1st		Receives 1 wagon limb G.S. for 19th but liquid hay. Receives one water cart for 6th Wilts Rgt	AP.O
	4th		Receives 1.18 pr Gun for 688 Bde R.F.A.	AP.O
	5th		Receives 1 G.S. wagon for 2 Lieut 19th D.L. Column	AP.O
	8th		Receives 1 G.S. wagon for 2 Sec. 19th A.Column. Receives 1 wagon L.S. for 5th So.Bord.	AP.O
	10th		Receives 2 water carts for 9th So.Lancs Regt. Receives 1 water cart for 58th Fd Ambce.	AP.O
	12th		Moves to St Jans Cappel	AP.O
	14th		Moved to Blaringhem	AP.O
	15th		Receives 1 wagon G.S. for 5th So. W. Borderers	AP.O
	17th		Receives 12 Lewis M.G. Junior Gun. Receives 1 wagon G.S. for 3 Lieut L.A. Column	AP.O
	19th		Receives 1 water cart for 7th Regt: Fan and 1 for 8th R. Staffords: Recd 1 Malted cart for 16th Worcesters	AP.O
	20th		Receives 8 Gretole Sig. 173" one for each Battery (WO.2955)	AP.O
	?		Receives 2.18 pr Guns, one for V/88 Bde and one for 6/87 Bde R.F.A.	AP.O
	22nd		Receives 1 cart water for V/88 Bde R.F.A.	AP.O
	25th		Receives 1 water cart for A/88 Bde R.F.A. Receives 1 water cart for 3 Lieut B.A.C.	AP.O
	28th		Receives 3 German Machine Guns and 4 German Rifles for Div. purposes	AP.O
	29th		Receives 2 G.S. wagons for Machine G.Column	AP.O
	29th		Receives 1500 bandoliers for field for Bde Regiments to replace old pattern in reserve	AP.O

A.J.Dodds.
Lieut. 19 ??
R.C. ?? 19 ??
3 D. 11 17

CONFIDENTIAL
WAR DIARY
OF
D.A.D.O.S. 19th Division
FROM 1st TO 31st DECEMBER 1917.

Army Form C. 2118

WAR DIARY
or
INTELLIGENCE SUMMARY
(Erase heading not required.)

Instructions regarding War Diaries and Intelligence Summaries are contained in F. S. Regs., Part II. and the Staff Manual respectively. Title Pages will be prepared in manuscript.

Place	Date	Hour	Summary of Events and Information	Remarks and references to Appendices
	1917. December			
	1st		Received 1 Water cart for 9th Bty. W.S. Fuero. Receives 1. 18 pdr gun for C/87 Bde. R.F.A.	App.
	6th		Moved to Basseux.	App.
	8th		Moved to Achiet le Petit.	App.
	10th		Moved to Ytres.	App.
	11th		Moved to Sericourt.	App.
	14th		Moved to Renville.	App.
	17th		Receives 1 Limber wagon for 112 Bty. R.F.A.	App.
	20th		Receives 1 G.S. Wagon for 53 Bty. R.F.A.	App.
	24th		Receives 1000 prs Thigh Boots	App.

A.J.Roberts
Lieut
R.D.A.O. 19th Div
31.12.17.

CONFIDENTIAL

WAR DIARY

OF

DADOS 19th DIVISION

FROM 1st TO 31st JANUARY

1918

Army Form C. 2118

WAR DIARY
or
INTELLIGENCE SUMMARY
(Erase heading not required.)

Instructions regarding War Diaries and Intelligence Summaries are contained in F.S. Regs., Part II. and the Staff Manual respectively. Title Pages will be prepared in manuscript.

Place	Date	Hour	Summary of Events and Information	Remarks and references to Appendices
	January 1916			
	1st		Received 1 Wagon Limbered G.S. for 9th Welsh Regt	A/P.O
	7th		Received 1 Wagon G.S. for No 1 Section 19 DAC + 1 Maltese Cart for C.R.E. 19th Division	A/P.O
	25th		Received 1-18 Pdr Gun for B.87 Bde R.F.A. and 1-18 Pdr Gun for B.68 Bde R.F.A.	A/P.O
	29th		Received 1 Watercart for 7th E. Lancs Regt, and 1 Travelling Kitchen for 5th S. Wales Borders	A/P.O

N. F. Ardale
Lieut
DADOS 19th Division
31-1-1918

CONFIDENTIAL

WAR DIARY

OF

D.A.D.O.S 19ᵗʰ DIVISION

FROM 1ˢᵀ TO 28ᵀᴴ FEBRUARY

1918.

Army Form C. 2118

WAR DIARY
or
INTELLIGENCE SUMMARY
(Erase heading not required.)

Instructions regarding War Diaries and Intelligence Summaries are contained in F.S. Regs, Part II. and the Staff Manual respectively. Title Pages will be prepared in manuscript.

Place	Date	Hour	Summary of Events and Information	Remarks and references to Appendices
	6th		Received 1 Vickers gun for 58th Machine Gun Coy	
	8th		Received 1 Watercart for 246th Machine Gun Coy, 1 Wagon limbered RE Body for 115th Army Coy and 1 Wagon limber M/S hind for 58th N. Staffs Regt.	
	10th		Received 8 Gunns Gun for Batteries RFA for A.A. purposes	
	15th		Moved to Le TRANSLOY. Received 1 Watercart for 11th Foshun Coy, 1 Kitchen Travelling Body for 9th Cheshire Regt, and 1 Wagon limbered RE Body for 91st Field Coy RE.	
	20th		Received 18 Gunns Gun for Infantry Battns for A.A. purposes	
	22nd		Received 1 Watercart for 8th N. Staffs Regt. and 1 Body Kitchen Travelling for 1/1 K.S.L.I.	
	23rd		Received 3 Gunns Guns for Field Coys RE. for A.A. purposes.	

A. G. Protte, Lieut
for DADTS 19th Division
28-2-1918

CONFIDENTIAL

WAR DIARY

OF

D.A.D.O.S 19TH DIVISION

FROM 1ST TO 31ST MARCH

1918

WAR DIARY
or
INTELLIGENCE SUMMARY

(Erase heading not required.)

Army Form C. 2118

Place	Date	Hour	Summary of Events and Information	Remarks and references to Appendices
	March 1918			
	4th		Received 26 Lewis Guns and 5 Hotchkiss Guns for A.A. purposes	APR
	6th		Received 1 Body Kitchen Travelling for 9th R. Welsh Fus, 1 Watercart each for 8th N. Staffs Regt and 8th Gloucester Regt, 1 Wagon Limbered G.S. for 5th/6th Water Bowser, 1 Wagon Pontoon for 6th P.J. (heavy R.E.) 1 Wagon Limb G.S. for 57th PJ Ambulance	APR
	10th		Received 1 Maw Cart neck for H.B 87½ Bde R.F.A. & 5th S. Water Bowser	APR
	23rd		Moved to POZIERES	APR
	25th		Moved to HEDAUVILLE	APR
	26th		Moved to LA CLOSERIE FARM	APR
	27th		Moved to BOUQUEMAISON	APR
	28th		Moved to PERNES	APR
	29th		Moved to ARQUES	APR
	30th		Moved to DRANOUTRE	APR
	31st		Received 114 Lewis Guns, 50 Vickers Guns, and 8 - 3 inch Stokes Munitions	APR

R.P.Smith
Captain
D.A.D.O.S. 19th Division

31-3-1918.

Confidential
War Diary
of
D.A.D.O.S. 19th Division
From 1st to 30th April
1918

WAR DIARY
or
INTELLIGENCE SUMMARY
(Erase heading not required.)

Army Form C. 2118

Instructions regarding War Diaries and Intelligence Summaries are contained in F. S. Regs., Part II. and the Staff Manual respectively. Title Pages will be prepared in manuscript.

Place	Date	Hour	Summary of Events and Information	Remarks and references to Appendices
	April 1916			
	1st		Moved to S, 17, D.7.1. Street 28 & Nilson 3.	1990
	3rd		Received 2 G.S. Wagons for 2 Coy. 19 Div Train, 1 Kitchen Trans + 1 Wagon Limbered G.S. for 9th Cheshire Regt, and 2 Kitchen Travelling Bodies for 7th K.S.L.I.	1990
	4th		Received 1-18 pdr. Gun Carriage for A.87 RFA, 1-18 pdr Gun Team for B.87, 2-18 pdrs Gun Team for C.87, 1-18 pdr Gun and Carr. for A.88, 1-18 pdr Gun Team for B.88, 2-18 pdr Gun Team for C.88, 1-4.5" How Team for D.88.	1990
	5th		Received 2-6" Newton Mortars for X.19 T.M.B, and 2 for Y.19 T.M.B, Limbers 18 pr Carr 2, Wagons 3 for A.87, Limbers 18 pr Carr. 6, Wagons 3 for B.87, Limbers 18 prs Carr 4 for A.88, Wagons Ammn 18 pr. 4 for A.87, 3, C.88, 1 D.88, 2.A.88, 2.C.88, Limbers 4.5", Carr. 1, Wagon 3, Wagons Ammn 4.5" H, for D.87, 1 Ambulance Horse for 3rd West Yorks, 1 Watercart for each A.88, 7th KSLI, 8 N Staffs, 19 M.Gun Coy, 2 Fire / Hand Wag Limb G.S. for 8th Long Rif, 1 Cart Mess each for H.B.87, H.B.88, C.87 RFA, 1 Wheeler Cart for each H.B. 87 + 88 Bag RFA, 1 Kitchen Trav. each for 10th Worceter + 8th Gloucester Regt, 1 Body Kitchen Trav each for 9th Cheshire + 10th R. Warwick Regt.	1990
	7th		Received 2 G.S. Wagons for N°1 Coy 19 Div Train, 8 G.S Wagons for 2 Sec 19 D.A.C. Received for D.87 RFA Limbers 4.5" How Carr. 1, Wagons 3, Wagons Ammn 4.5" How H.	1990
	8th		Received 1 G.S. Wagon for 1 Sec 19 DAC, 1 Watercart + 1 Kitchen Trav. for H.B.87 Inf Bde, 1 Kitchen Body for 9th Welsh Regt, 2 Kitchen Bodies for 9th Cheshire Regt, 6 Wagon Ammn 18 pr, 2 Limbers Wagon 18 pr. for 2 Sec 19 DAC.	1990
	9th		Received 1 CWC Wagon for D.88. RFA	1990
	10th		Moved to BERTHEN. Received 1 Kitchen Trans for H.B.87 Inf Bde., 1 Kitchen Limber for 8 N.Staff Regt, 1 Cart Mess for B.87 RFA	1990
	11th		Received 5 G.S. Wagons for 1 Sec 19 D.A.C, 4 & 2 for 3 Sec 19 DAC, 1 Kitchen Body for 8th N Staff Regt.	1990

WAR DIARY
or
INTELLIGENCE SUMMARY

Sheet 2.

Army Form C. 2118

Place	Date Hour	Summary of Events and Information	Remarks and references to Appendices
	April 1915		
	12th	Moved to BEAUVOORDE	MD
	14th	Received 13 Wagons limbered G.S. for 3 Sec 19th D.A.C., and 2 for 109 R.E. Warwick Regt, 1 Watercart for 9th RWF &c	MD
	15th	Received 1-4.5" How-carriage for D 87 RFA	MD
	18th	Received 6-16pr Gun-carriages for C.88 RFA.	MD
	20th	Received 1 Watercart each for 9th Welsh Regt, + 10th R.E. Warwick Regt, 1 Hind part Wag Limb G.S for each H&B 87 RFA, 6 Wks Regt, 2 Fore parts Wag Limb G.S for 9th Welsh Regt, 1-4.5" How-carriage for D.86 RFA, 1-18pr Gun-Carr for A 87 RFA.	MD
	21st	Moved to PROVEN. Received 1D Lewis guns for 9th R.W. Fus + 3 for 11th K.S.L.I.	MD
	22nd	Received 7 Lewis guns for 9th Cheshire Regt, 1-18pd Gun-Carriage for A 87 RFA, 1 Limber Wagon 16pr to B 88, 1 Watercarts + 1 Amm. Wagon Limb. G.S. for 11th K.S.L.I.	MD
	23	Received 1 Wagon Limb G.S. for 9th R.E. Cav R.E., 1 Amm Cart for D.88, 1 Watercart for 9th R.E. Cav R.E.,	MD
	24th	Received 1th Lewis guns for 6th Wilts Regt, 1 Body, Kitchen Travelling for 9th Wilts Regt.	MD
	27th	Moved to K.1.D.B.8.6 Sheet 27. Received 3 Wagons Amm 16pr, 1 Limber Gun + 1 Limber Wagon 18pr to	MD
	28th	C.86 RFA, 5 Wagons Ammn, 4 Limber Wagons 16pr. for 3 Sec 19th D.A.C.	MD
	30th	Received 1 Hind Wag Limb G.S. to 5 A/5 P.S. Amble, 2 Fore, 6 Hind Wag Limb G.S. for 19th M.G. Battery, 1 Watercart A 87 RFA, 1 Wagon Ammn 16pr. A 87, 2 Wagons Ammn 16pr A 87, 3 Wagons Ammn 16pr 1 Amm Cart each H&B 87 RFA + C 87 RFA	MD

A.J. Dodds
Captain
DADOS 19th Division
2-5-1915

CONFIDENTIAL

War Diary

of

D.A.D.O.S. 19th Division

From 1st to 31st May 1918

No. 34

WAR DIARY
or
INTELLIGENCE SUMMARY

Army Form C. 2118

(Erase heading not required.)

Instructions regarding War Diaries and Intelligence Summaries are contained in F. S. Regs., Part II. and the Staff Manual respectively. Title Pages will be prepared in manuscript.

Place	Date May 1916	Hour	Summary of Events and Information	Remarks and references to Appendices
	1st		Received 7 – 3 inch Stokes mortars for 57th Trench Mortar Battery	App.
	3rd		Received 6 Lewis guns for 5th South Wales Borderers	App.
	7th		Received 1 Watercart for each 9th Cheshire Regt and 9th Welsh Regt., 1 Kitchen Body for 9th Welsh Regt. 1 Limber G.S. hind for 9th Welsh Regt., 1 Wagon Limbered G.S. for N.H. 1st Coy R.E., 1 Wagon Pontoon for 83rd Fd Coy R.E.	App.
	10th		Received 10 Vickers Guns for 19th Machine Gun Battalion	App.
	11th		Received 4 Vickers guns for 19th M.G. un Battn., 4 Lewis guns each for 10th Rl. Warwick, 15th Worcester, & 10th Gloucester Regts., 1 Watercart for 9th Fd Coy R.E., 1 Kitchen Body for 5/5 W. un Borders	App.
	17th		Moved to St Gervais-La-Ville	App.
	29th		Moved to Cardonny	App.
	31st		Moved to Domeny. Received 1 Limber 16 pdr Wagon, 1 Wagon Ammn 18pr, 1 Watercart for B 67 R.F.A., 1 Wagon Limb Aid for 10th Rl Warwick Regt., 1 Wagon Limb Fire for H.B. 57 Rde., 1 Fore, 2 Hind Wagons Limbered G.S. for 19th M Gun Battn.	App.

P.J. Dodds
Captain
D.A.D.O.S 19th Division

31-5-16

Army Form C. 2118

WAR DIARY
or
INTELLIGENCE SUMMARY
(Erase heading not required.)

Instructions regarding War Diaries and Intelligence Summaries are contained in F. S. Regs., Part II. and the Staff Manual respectively. Title Pages will be prepared in manuscript.

Place	Date	Hour	Summary of Events and Information	Remarks and references to Appendices
	May 1916			
	1st		Received 7 - 3 inch Stokes Mortars for 57th Trench Mortar Battery	A930
	3rd		Received 6 Lewis Guns for 5th South Wales Borderers	A930
	7th		Received 1 Watercart for each 9th Cheshire Regt and 9th Welsh Regt, 1 Kitchen Body for 5th Wilts Regt, 1 Limber G.S. limb for 9th Welsh Regt, 1 Wagon Limbered G.S. for 9th & 8 Coy R.E., 1 Wagon Pontoon for 82nd Ft Coy R.E.	A930
	10th		Received 10 Vickers Guns for 19th Machine Gun Battalion	A930
	11th		Received 4 Vickers Guns for 19th MG un Batn, 4 Lewis Guns each for 10th R.E. Warwick, 11th Worcester & 5th Gloucester Regts, 1 Watercart for 9th Ft Coy R.E., 1 Kitchen Body for 5th S Wales Borders	A930
	17th		Moved to St Germain-La-Ville	A930
	24th		Moved to Cachenry	A930
	31st		Moved to Daours. Received 1 Limber, 16 pdr Wagon, 1 Wagon Ammn 18 pdr, 1 Watercart for B 67 R.F.A, 1 Wagon Limb Amd for 1st R.O. Warwick Regt, 1 Wagon Limb For for H.B.S. 57 Bde, 1 For. & Mur. Wagon Limbered G.S. for 19th M Gun Battn	A930

A.J. Brady
Captain
A.D.S.S. 19th Division
31-5-16

CONFIDENTIAL

WAR DIARY

OF

DADOS 19TH DIVISION

FROM 1ST April TO 30TH JUNE

1918

Army Form C. 2118

WAR DIARY
or
INTELLIGENCE SUMMARY
(Erase heading not required.)

Instructions regarding War Diaries and Intelligence Summaries are contained in F. S. Regs., Part II. and the Staff Manual respectively. Title Pages will be prepared in manuscript.

Date	Hour	Summary of Events and Information	Remarks and references to Appendices
June 1916			
2nd		Moved to Cujs.	App.
3rd		Received 13 Vickers guns for 19th M. Gun Battalion	App.
7th		Received 3 Pairs, 6 Hind Wagons numbered G.S. for 19th M.G. Battery, 1 Hind Wagon Limber G.S. for 5 gun 1st Queens	App.
11th		Received 16 Service guns for 4th Welsh Regt, and 16 for 2nd Wilts Regt.	App.
12th		Received 1 Water Cart and 1 Kitchen for 2nd Wilts Regt, 1 G.S. Wagon Limber G.S. for 5 1/8 S.W.B., 1 Wagon Limber G.S. Complete for 4th Coy R.E., 1 Wagon G.S. for No.1 Coy 19th Div Train, 1 Wagon G.S. + Wagons Ammun H.3. Horses for No.1 Sec 19th D.A.C.	App.
13th		Received 16 Lewis guns for 9th Rl. Welsh Fusiliers	App.
19th		Moved to MONDEMENT. Received 1 Cook Cart for use H.867, 186 RFA, A.87 and 287 RFA, and 2 Wagons G.S. for No.1 Sec. 19th D.A.C.	App.
20th		Received 4 Vickers Guns for 119th M. Gun Battalion	App.
21st		Received 5 Vickers Guns for 19th M. Gun Batn, and 48 Lewis Guns for Infantry Battalions	App.
24th		Received 1 G.S. Wagon for No.1 Sec.19 DAC, 1 Watercart + Muffle Cart for 582 Rl. Queens, 2 Pair, 1 Hind Wagon	App.
27th		Limbered G.S. for S.A.A. Sec 19 DAC, 1 Watercart for A.67, 3 Complete Kitchens Travelling 1 K.T. Body + 1 Watercart for 5th Worcester Regt.	App.

A.J. Sedds
Captain
DADOS 19th Division
20.7.1916

CONFIDENTIAL

WAR DIARY

OF

D.A.D.O.S. 19TH DIVISION

FROM 1ST TO 31ST JULY

1918

Army Form C. 2118

WAR DIARY
or
INTELLIGENCE SUMMARY
(Erase heading not required.)

Instructions regarding War Diaries and Intelligence Summaries are contained in F. S. Regs., Part II. and the Staff Manual respectively. Title Pages will be prepared in manuscript.

Place	Date	Hour	Summary of Events and Information	Remarks and references to Appendices
	JULY 1916			
	4th		Moved to FAUQUENBERGUES	
	9th		Received 2 Wagons Ammunition 18 pdr; & 2 Limbers 18pdr for N⁰1 Sec 19 DAC. 1 Limber Wagon 18 pdr for N⁰2 Sec 19 DAC.	
	19th		Moved to BELLERY. Received 1 Limber Wagon Cable & 1 Wagon Limbered RE Body for 19 Signal Coy RE, 1 Wagon Limbered G.S. for 5th S.W. Borderers.	
	20th		Received 1 Lewis gun for each 6th, 60th, & 9th & 11th Coy R.E.	
	22nd		Received 2 Watercarts & 1 G.S. Wagon for 19th M.Gun Coy (Baty). 1 Watercart for 11 Coy 19th Divis Train A.S.C.	
	23rd		Received 1 G.S. Wagon for N⁰1 Section 19th D.A.C.	
	24th		Received 1 Watercart for 9th Rl Welsh Fusiliers	
	25th		Received 12 Lewis guns for Infantry Battns, 1 Limber, & 2 Bodies Wagon Cable for 19 Sig Coy R.E.	
	27th		Received 1 Kitchen Travelling Body for 8th Gloucester Regt.	

A. G. Bishop
Lieut
for D.A.D.O.S. 19th Division
31-7-1916

CONFIDENTIAL
WAR DIARY
OF
D.A.D.O.S. 19TH DIVISION
FROM 1ST TO 31ST AUGUST
1918

Army Form C. 2118

WAR DIARY
or
INTELLIGENCE SUMMARY
(Erase heading not required.)

Instructions regarding War Diaries and Intelligence Summaries are contained in F.S. Regs., Part II. and the Staff Manual respectively. Title Pages will be prepared in manuscript.

Place	Date	Hour	Summary of Events and Information	Remarks and references to Appendices
	August 1915			
	1st		Received 12 Lewis Guns for 1/7th R. Welsh Fus., 11 for 3rd Monmouth Regt., and 14 for 8th Gloucester Regt.	APP.
	2nd		Received 1 G.S. Wagon for 1/3rd M.G. un Battery, 1 Pontoon Wagon for 2/1st Field Coy. R.E.	APP.
	3rd		Received 1 - 18 pdr Gun for B, 87 Brigade, R.F.A.	APP.
	6th		Moved to D.11.D.2.9. Sheet 44.B	APP.
	16th		Received 1 G.S. Wagon and 1 Wagon Limbered G.S. for S.A.A. Section 1/1st D.A.C.	APP.
	17th		Received 1 Limber Wagon + 1 Wagon Ammunition 11.6" How? for D.88. R.F.A.	APP.
	19th		Received 1 Wagon Limbered G.S. Fire for H.883 5th Bn. Sct. 64th	APP.
	20th		Received 2 Vickers Guns for 1/9th Bn. Gun Battalion	APP.
	24th		Moved to ALLOUAGNE. Received 1 - 4.5" How? and Carriage for D.118.R.F.A.	APP.
	26th		Received 1 - 18 pdr Gun for A, 66 R.F.A.	APP.
	30th		Received 1 G.S. Wagon for N.2. Section 1/1st D.A.C.	

A.J. Antcliff
Major
D.A.D.O.S., 1st Division
31-8-1915

CONFIDENTIAL

WAR DIARY
of
D.A.D.O.S. 19th DIVISION
FROM 1st TO 30th SEPTEMBER
1918

WAR DIARY
or
INTELLIGENCE SUMMARY
(Erase heading not required.)

Army Form C. 2118

Place	Date	Hour	Summary of Events and Information	Remarks and references to Appendices
	Sept 1915			
	2nd		Received 1 Waistcoat for B. 87 RFA	
	6th		Moved to BETHUNE. Received 1-4.5" How. Carriage for D. 87 RFA	
	10th		Received 1-Wagon Ammn 18pdr for A. 117 RFA	
	12th		Received 1 Wagon Limbered G.S. for O/C Field Coy R.E. and 1 Wagon G.S. for №3 Section 19th D.A.C.	
	15th		Received 1-18pdr Gun and Carriage for A. 87 RFA	
	17th		Received 3 Vickers Guns for 1st M. Gun Battery, 1-4.5" How Carriage for D. 46 RFA, 1 GS Wagon 3 for 19 DAC	
	19th		Received 1 Carriage 18pdr for B. 68 RFA, 1-15pdr Gun Carriage for C. 88 RFA, 1 Wagon G.S. 1 sec 19 DAC	
	20th		Received 1 GS Wagon for Rev 19 DAC	
	21st		Received 1 Kitchen Travelling for GHQ, N. 083, 1-8" Stokes Mortar for 568 T.M. Battery	
	23rd		Received 11 Lewis Guns for O/b Rg RG Warwick Reg.	
	24th		Received 1 Wagon Limbered G.S. for B Section 19 D.A.C.	
	26th		Received 1-8" Stokes Mortar for 575 T.M. Battery	
	28th		Received 1 Vickers Gun for 1st M. Gun Battery	

A.G. R. Lt. Sinne
for DADOS 19th Division
30.9.1915

CONFIDENTIAL
WAR DIARY
OF
D.A.D.O.S. 19th DIVISION
FROM 1st TO 31st OCTOBER 1918.

Army Form C. 2118

WAR DIARY
or
INTELLIGENCE SUMMARY
(Erase heading not required.)

Instructions regarding War Diaries and Intelligence Summaries are contained in F. S. Regs., Part II. and the Staff Manual respectively. Title Pages will be prepared in manuscript.

Place	Date	Hour	Summary of Events and Information	Remarks and references to Appendices
	October 1916			
	1st		Received 1 Wagon Ammn 18 pdr for A. 87 Bty RFA.	App.
	4th		Moved to LA HERLIÈRE	App.
	7th		Moved to GRAINCOURT	App.
	9th		Moved to NOYELLES	App.
	10th		Received 1 Vickers Gun for 1/9th M.G. Bde, 1 Lewis Gun each for 10th R.E. Warwick, 2nd Worcester, 9th Cheshire Regts and 3 for 8th Gloucester Regt	App.
	13th		Moved to CAMBRAI	App.
	15th		Moved to AVESNES LES AUBERT	App.
	22nd		Received 1 Wagon Limbered G.S. Fore for 1/4th Fd Coy RE, 1 Cart wheeler + 1 Wagon Limbered G.S. for 1st Signal Coy RE, 1 Kitchen Trav Limber for 5th S.W.B., 1 Kitchen Trav Body each for 9th Cheshire + 8th N. Staffs Regts	App.
	27th		Received 1 Limbert 2 Bodies Kitchen Travelling for 5th Welsh Regt, 1 Wagon Limbered G.S. Fore for 19th M.G. Bde	App.
	28th		Received 1 Lewis Gun each for 2nd Wilts Regt and 9th R.E. Welsh Fusiliers.	App.
	31st		Received 10 Wagons Limbered G.S. Fore 3, Hind 1. for 9th Cheshire Regt	App.

Major
DADTS (?) Division

CONFIDENTIAL
WAR DIARY
OF
D.A.D.O.S. 19th DIVISION
FROM 1st TO 30th NOVEMBER
1918

Army Form C. 2118

WAR DIARY
or
INTELLIGENCE SUMMARY
(Erase heading not required.)

Instructions regarding War Diaries and Intelligence Summaries are contained in F.S. Regs., Part II. and the Staff Manual respectively. Title Pages will be prepared in manuscript.

Place	Date November 1918	Hour	Summary of Events and Information	Remarks and references to Appendices
	1st		Received 1-18pdr Gun for A.67.R.F.A, 1 Watercart for D.67 R.F.A, + 1 Wagon Cable Limber for 19 Signal Coy R.E	APD
	3rd		Moved to VENDEGIES-SUR-ECAILLON.	APD
	4th		Moved to JENLAIN	APD
	5th		Received 2 Lewis Guns for 9th Cheshire Regt.	APD
	9th		Received 1-4.5" Carriage for D.67. R.F.A.	APD
	10th		Received 1 Kitchen Travelling Body for each of 9th R.Welsh Fus. & 3rd Worcester Regt., 2 complete Wagon Limbered G.S. for 9th R.Welsh Fus., + 1 for 19th Machine Gun Battalion.	APD
	12th		Moved to AVESNES-LEZ-AUBERT	APD
	14th		Received 3 complete Wagon Limbered G.S. for S.A.A. Section 19th D.A.C., 1 Hand Pack Wagon Limbered G.S. for H.Q. 5th Inf. Bde.	APD
	21st			APD
	26th		Moved to NADURS.	APD
	28th		Received 1 Watercart for C.68. R.F.A., + 1 Maun Cart for 10th R. Warwick Regt.	APD

A J Dodds
Major
D.A.D.O.S. 19th Division
30-11-18

CONFIDENTIAL WAR DIARY

OF

D.A.D.O.S. 19th DIVISION

FROM 1st TO 31st DECEMBER 1918

Army Form C. 2118

WAR DIARY
or
INTELLIGENCE SUMMARY
(Erase heading not required.)

Instructions regarding War Diaries and Intelligence Summaries are contained in F.S. Regs., Part II. and the Staff Manual respectively. Title Pages will be prepared in manuscript.

Place	Date	Hour	Summary of Events and Information	Remarks and references to Appendices
	December 1918			
	6th		Received 2 Wagons Amm. Q.F. 4.5" Howitzers for D/187 Bde R.F.A.	APD
	9th		Moved to DANDAS.	APD
	15*		1 Wagon G.S. received for 232 A.F.A. Bde Amm Col	APD
	21		Received 1 Water Cart for 19th Hyrical boy & 1 K.T. brody for 1040 Warwicks	APD

A F Dodds.
Major
DANDAS, 19 Dec
31-12-18.

CONFIDENTIAL
WAR DIARY
OF
D.A.D.O.S 19ᵗʰ DIVISION
FROM 1ˢᵗ TO 31ˢᵗ JANUARY
1919

WAR DIARY
or
INTELLIGENCE SUMMARY

Army Form C. 2118

(Erase heading not required.)

Place	Date	Hour	Summary of Events and Information	Remarks and references to Appendices
	January 1916			
	15th		Received 2 Kitchen Travelling Bodies for 10th Royal Warwick Regt.	
	27th		Received 1 Waggon for D.66 & 78th R.F.A.	

A. J. Porter
Major
DADOS 10th Division
1-2-1916

CONFIDENTIAL

WAR DIARY

OF

D.A.D.O.S. 19th Division

From 1st To 28th February

1919

WAR DIARY
or
INTELLIGENCE SUMMARY

(Erase heading not required.)

Army Form C. 2118

Place	Date	Hour	Summary of Events and Information	Remarks and references to Appendices
	February 1919		Nil	

A.J. Andels
Major
D.A.D.S.S. ADMD
26.2.1919

www.ingramcontent.com/pod-product-compliance
Lightning Source LLC
Chambersburg PA
CBHW081437160426
43193CB00013B/2303